The anti-ageing cookbook
with over 70 recipes

ROBYN MARTIN

TED SMART

I dedicate this book to my dad. If only he had known what I have learnt, he may have had a long and healthy life reaping the happiness of his family's love, sharing their achievements and milestones.

Life inspires us to grow into our future, to challenge our genetics and never accept that we do not have the power to make a change.
Samuel James Matthews 3 May 1923 – 14 May 1992

A special thanks to Professor John Birkbeck for his assistance in checking the claims made in this book.

First published in 2004 by Random House New Zealand

This edition published in 2006 for The Book People Ltd, Hall Wood Avenue, Haydock, St Helens WA11 9UL

1 3 5 7 9 10 8 6 4 2

Random House UK Ltd, Random House, Vauxhall Bridge Road, London SW1V 2SA

Random House Australia (Pty) Limited
20 Alfred Street, Milsons Point, Sydney, New South Wales 2061, Australia

Random House New Zealand Limited
18 Poland Road, Glenfield, Auckland 10, New Zealand

Random House South Africa (Pty) Limited
Isle of Houghton Corner Boundary Road & Carse O'Gowrie, Houghton , 2198, South Africa

Random House UK Limited Reg. No. 954009
www.randomhouse.co.uk

A CIP catalogue record for this book is available from the British Library

Photography: Alan Gillard
Recipes tested by Virginia Hewin and Rosemary Hurdley
Design: Richard Wheatley, Red Design Limited
Crockery supplied by Smith & Caughey Limited

ISBN: 0 091 91026 9

Papers used by Ebury are natural, recyclable products made from wood grown in sustainable forests.

Printed and bound in Singapore by Tien Wah Press

contents

introduction

We have all had a taste of the good life, those of us that enjoyed growing up in the Forties, Fifties and Sixties. We shocked our families with the freedoms of the Sixties, Seventies and Eighties and had our halcyon days forging a path in life and careers. We renovated the odd bungalow or villa along the way, had the babies, watched governments come and go, and now we have been put on a treadmill to miraculously stash away something for the third age – whatever that may be.

Amid all this, we still have a huge amount we want to do and we want to be able to do it in full working order. We all want to defy the ageing process and get the most out of life. We want everything operating at its peak. The blunt and wonderful truth is we do not want to grow old. We want to have lots more birthdays and a fantastic quality of life that enables us to enjoy the new experiences and wisdom that come with age.

More and more we hear that we are what we eat. If you have had a poor diet you are probably feeling the effects of it now. The simple truth is that it is never too late to try to arrest the ravages of time and in some cases it is even possible to make amends.

The ageing antidotes included in each chapter of this book are intended to

highlight the importance of eating a wide variety of foods and emphasises foods of plant origin for their positive health benefits. No single food is the elixir of a long and healthy life. Instead, think of foods working together in a big chemical reaction to give your body the maximum possible health and anti-ageing benefits. Making sure that chemical reaction is as beneficial as it possibly can be comes down to choosing the right foods.

This book is about eating the foods that will do just that – foods that will help slow the tick-tock of the clock. Many recipes have ingredients with a multitude of anti-ageing benefits and the lists of foods at the beginning of each chapter will help you identify them.

This is a book that is all about making our food choices count, to defy the ageing process with knowledge and enthusiasm, making sure we do get the most out of life.

To life!

important ingredients
to improve brain function

tuna	cabbage	nuts
salmon	spinach	flaxseed oil
sardines	broccoli	turmeric
anchovies	potatoes	ginkgo
chicken	soya beans	coffee
strawberries	soya milk	red wine
blueberries	tofu	beer
beetroot	tempeh	
tomatoes	miso	

the brain drain

I am probably speaking for many people of our generation, so aptly named the baby boomers, when I say that the thought of losing my marbles to Alzheimer's or another dementia sends chills down my spine.

Many of us have seen the demise of fine minds to these diseases. Some will even have nursed a loved one through the perils of a failing mind. None of us wants to go there – it is one tee-shirt we do not need.

The good news is that there are many everyday foods that have been proven to slow the degeneration of the brain caused by ageing. If you know what they are it is easy to incorporate them into the list of foods you choose to eat regularly.

There is much research being done in this area and when new claims are made, take them on board. This is one part of the body for which surgical repair is not an option.

Straw-Blue Fruit Smoothie

Now don't turn your nose up at this. Smoothies are not just for youth! Try this for breakfast or, if you can't cope with that, perhaps have it as a snack with a sandwich at lunch or, at worst, use it as a cocktail base for that pre-dinner drink.

8–10 fresh or frozen strawberries
1 banana
75g fresh or frozen blueberries
1 tablespoon flaxseed oil
6 whole blanched almonds
2 tablespoons oat bran
125ml skim milk or low-fat soya milk or fresh orange juice

Hull strawberries. Peel banana. Place strawberries, banana, blueberries, flaxseed oil, almonds and oat bran in a blender and blend until smooth. Add milk and blend. Serve chilled.

Serves 1

Blueberries have been found to reverse some aspects of brain ageing in animal studies. From a human perspective they are a no-risk way of having a crack at achieving the same result – try eating a handful a day and see the benefits.

When we use our brain we use energy, and one-third more oxygen than other body functions. This produces free radicals. We need antioxidants to scoop up these free radicals to prevent them damaging our brain. Berry fruit all have high levels of antioxidants. Blueberries, blackberries, cranberries, strawberries and raspberries provide wonderful protection for the brain.

Beetroot contains a host of beneficial vitamins, minerals and other compounds that help to energise the body and improve memory and concentration. These include beta-carotene (this is converted to vitamin A in the body), folic acid, vitamins B6 and C, manganese, calcium, magnesium, iron, potassium and phosphorus. Beetroot leaves are the best source of these nutrients.

Beetroot contains powerful antioxidants that help scoop up the free radicals, which have an adverse effect on brain ageing. It is also thought to improve memory and concentration.

Beetroot, Spinach and Broccoli Salad

1 head broccoli
2 medium beetroot
2 large handfuls baby spinach
80g shelled pistachio nuts
3 tablespoons avocado oil
1 tablespoon red wine vinegar
freshly ground black pepper

Wash broccoli and cut into florets. Pour boiling water over broccoli and leave for 5 minutes. Drain and refresh under cold water and drain again. Peel beetroot and grate coarsely. Arrange washed spinach leaves over the base of a bowl or serving platter. Top with grated beetroot. Scatter over broccoli and pistachio nuts. Drizzle over avocado oil and vinegar. Grind over black pepper and serve.

Serves 6

Chicken and Vegetable Soup

1 onion
2 cloves garlic
1 tablespoon avocado oil
1 litre chicken stock
1 medium sweet potato
1 bunch spinach
1 head broccoli
1 carrot
200g boneless, skinless chicken
2 tomatoes

Peel onion and chop finely. Crush garlic, peel and chop finely. Heat avocado oil in a large saucepan and sauté onion and garlic for 5 minutes until clear but not coloured. Add chicken stock and bring to the boil. Peel sweet potato. Cut into chunks and add to stock mixture. Cover and cook for 10 minutes or until sweet potato is cooked. Wash and trim spinach. Wash broccoli and cut into small florets. Scrub carrot and cut into slices. Cut chicken into bite-sized pieces. Cut tomatoes into small cubes. When sweet potato is cooked, mash coarsely in the liquid with a potato masher. Bring to the boil and add spinach, broccoli, carrot and chicken. Cook for 5 minutes or until chicken is cooked. Serve topped with chopped tomatoes.

Serves 4

Carrots have a high level of beta-carotene, which converts to vitamin A in the body. They are being investigated for their help in retaining memory, because the area of the brain that specialises in memory function cannot operate without vitamin A.

Broccoli is an excellent source of lipoic acid, which is claimed to increase energy and brain power. Tomatoes are also a good source of lipoic acid.

Curcumin, the pigment that makes turmeric yellow, has a powerful anti-inflammatory effect. Inflammation is being investigated as a possible contributor to Alzheimer's disease. Turmeric has also been shown to reduce plaques in the brain that cause Alzheimer's disease.

The long-chain omega-3 fatty acids found in fish oils are essential for normal brain function.

Fish Cakes with Indian Tomato Sauce

If you don't have Thai green curry paste, use curry powder. Stir it into the onions after they have cooked for 3 minutes.

>   200g can tuna in water
>   1 red onion
>   1 tablespoon oil
>   120g baby spinach
>   2 teaspoons turmeric
>   1 tablespoon ground linseeds
>   425g cold mashed potato
>   2 tablespoons Thai flavour base
>   2-3 teaspoons curry paste of your
>   favourite flavour
>   3 tablespoons olive oil
>   400g can chopped tomatoes

Drain tuna. Peel onion and chop finely. Heat oil in a frying pan and sauté onion over a medium heat for 5 minutes or until soft. Add washed spinach and turmeric and stir until spinach wilts. Mix tuna, onion mixture, linseeds, potato, curry paste and fish sauce together until well combined. Shape 100g portions of mixture into patties. Heat oil in a frying pan. Cook patties over a medium heat until lightly golden. Turn and cook second side. While patties are cooking, heat tomatoes. Serve patties with Indian tomatoes.

Serves 2-3

Smoked Salmon, Spinach and Egg Pies

2 sheets (500g) ready-rolled puff pastry (see below)
1 bunch spinach
200g wood-roasted smoked salmon
2 tablespoons capers
2 tablespoons chopped fresh dill
4 eggs

Cut each pastry sheet in half on the diagonal. Place on an oven tray. Wash spinach and trim. Pour boiling water over. Drain spinach, removing as much water as possible. Remove bones from salmon with clean tweezers and remove skin. Mix salmon, capers, dill and spinach together in a bowl. Divide mixture among the four pastry pieces, placing at the right-angled corner of the pastry triangle. Wet edges of pastry and fold points of long side over the filling to the right-angled point and seal. Open the slit in the middle of the pies and break an egg into each. Break the egg yolk with a knife. Bake at 200°C/Gas 7 for 25-30 minutes, or until pastry is golden and cooked.

Serves 4

Spinach is one of the better food sources of glutathione and alpha-lipoic acid, which are important antioxidants in the body. Glutathione is found in the watery cell interior. It protects the DNA in our cells from oxidation. Alpha-lipoic acid helps cells absorb an amino acid essential for the body to make glutathione. It helps strengthen the memory and turns off genes that can accelerate ageing.

Oily fish feature heavily in all aspects of anti-ageing health. Knowing the oil content of your favourite fish is important if your fish-eating objective is to have the advantage of omega-3 fatty acids in your diet.

To make linseed pastry, sprinkle rolled pastry with 1-2 tablespoons crushed linseeds, then roll a rolling pin over the surface to press them in.

Fish oils are essential for normal brain function. Low fish consumption has been linked to a range of psychiatric disorders.

Nuts are a good source of vitamin E, which acts as an antioxidant and helps prevent Alzheimer's disease.

Crusty Salmon with Grilled Tomatoes and Oregano

2 serving-sized pieces salmon fillet
35g chopped mixed nuts
2 tablespoons sun-dried tomato pesto
3 medium tomatoes
freshly ground black pepper
fresh oregano leaves
baby spinach leaves

Remove bones from salmon with clean tweezers and remove skin if preferred. Place fish on a piece of parchment paper on an oven tray. Mix nuts and pesto together. Spread over top surface of salmon. Cut tomatoes in half around the equator (not through stem end). Grind black pepper over cut surfaces and place on oven tray. Grill salmon and tomatoes for 5 minutes under a hot grill or in the oven at 200°C/Gas 6 until salmon is still slightly rare and tomatoes heated through. Sprinkle tomatoes with oregano and serve with baby spinach leaves.

Serves 2

Fresh Tuna Loin with Wasabi and Anchovy Mayo

400g piece fresh tuna loin
1 tablespoon avocado oil
1 teaspoon garlic salt
1 bunch spinach

Brush the tuna with avocado oil and sprinkle lightly with garlic salt. Grill or barbecue each side for 1 to 2 minutes depending on the thickness of the fish. (The inside of the tuna should be rare.) Cover and stand for 5 minutes. Wash spinach and cook in a saucepan with just the water clinging to the leaves for 2 to 3 minutes or until bright green and wilted. Drain, pressing out as much water as possible. Cut tuna into 0.5cm thick slices. Arrange on top of spinach and top with Wasabi and Anchovy Mayo.

Wasabi and Anchovy Mayo

50g tin anchovies in oil
125g low-fat mayonnaise
½ teaspoon wasabi powder
1 tablespoon chopped chives

Mash anchovies in 1 tablespoon of their oil. Mix in mayonnaise, wasabi and chives.

Serves 2

Fish oils help improve memory and brain function.

Fish that have high oil-content include anchovies, mackerel, mullet, sardines, salmon, sprats and albacore tuna.

Fish that have medium-to-high oil-content include orange roughy, skipjack and southern bluefin tuna, and marlin.

There are indications that blueberries can prevent or delay the onset of Alzheimer's disease.

Large amounts of alcohol kill brain cells.

Researchers have found that protein deposits form on the brains of people with Alzheimer's disease. Foods rich in vitamin E, such as wheatgerm, nuts and oils, are being studied for their role in preventing the formation of these protein deposits on the brain – another good reason to include vitamin E-rich foods in your diet.

Very Berry Sorbet

As you get older, one of the hardest things is to maintain your weight, so do your bit for God and the Queen and enjoy all the delicious foods we have on offer. Ice cream doesn't fit into a regular regime but a sorbet that packs a punch can make an enjoyable, delicious substitute. Try this for size.

500g mixture of fresh or free-flow frozen blueberries, strawberries, raspberries and blackberries
40ml lime cordial
250ml cup fresh orange juice
1 egg white

Mash fresh or frozen berries in a bowl. Mix in lime cordial and orange juice. Pour into a shallow freezerproof container. Freeze until almost solid. Turn into a food processor. Add egg white. (Alternatively, break frozen berry mixture into pieces in a bowl and add egg white.) Process or beat with a mixer until combined. Cover and refreeze until frozen. If you are going to store this in the freezer make sure the surface of the sorbet is covered with cling film to prevent ice crystals forming.

Serves 6

Fresh Berry Terrine

600ml cranberry juice
3 tablespoons gelatine
250g fresh or frozen raspberries
300g fresh or frozen blueberries
16 sponge fingers

Take 60ml from the measured cranberry juice. Sprinkle gelatine over and soak for 5 minutes. Dissolve in a bowl over hot water or in the microwave on High for 10 seconds. Stir into remaining cranberry juice. Mix in fresh or thawed berries. Line the base and sides of a straight-sided 1.5-litre dish with sponge fingers, rounded side out. Pour in fruit mixture. Cover and refrigerate until set. Trim ends of sponge fingers that are above jelly level. To serve, dip dish into hot water and turn out on to a serving plate. Serve with yoghurt or your favourite low-fat ice cream.

Serves 8

the brain drain

25

Buy fruits and vegetables with the best, brightest colour. If they are meant to be red, make sure you buy the brightest red – not half green. When fruits and vegetables are ripe they provide the optimum amount of antioxidants, minerals and vitamins. For example, blueberries can triple their level of natural antioxidants from the time they first turn blue to reaching full ripeness.

Research has shown that blueberries slow, and in some cases reverse, damage in ageing brains, improving short-term memory and co-ordination.

Fresh Blueberry Sauce

300g fresh blueberries
90g blueberry jam
3 tablespoons water

Place blueberries, jam and water in a blender or food processor. Blend or process until berries are lightly crushed.

Makes about 400ml

Chocolate contains powerful antioxidants called catechins and the secret to tapping into these antioxidants is to buy good-quality dark chocolate. The more cocoa solids in the chocolate, the greater the antioxidants present. Anything less that 35 per-cent chocolate and you are kidding yourself about the 'treat with a health benefit'.

Despite all the negatives said about coffee, having two to three cups a day reduces the risk of Alzheimer's disease.

Mocha Dessert Cake with Fresh Blueberry Sauce

Looking after your health doesn't mean you have to eat mung beans and chant. Nor do you have to become a health-food guru. The important ingredients for brain health can be incorporated in your diet with ease once you know what they are.

250ml boiling water
20g ground coffee
150g butter
100g dark chocolate
150g sugar
3 eggs
2 teaspoons vanilla essence
250g plain flour
2 teaspoons baking powder
1 teaspoon bicarbonate of soda
25g cocoa powder

Line the base of a deep, 20cm round cake tin with parchment paper. Pour water over coffee grounds in a plunger or jug. Leave for 5 minutes to steep. Plunge or strain coffee. Melt butter in a saucepan large enough to mix all the ingredients. Remove from heat. Mix in chocolate and coffee and stir to melt chocolate. Add sugar, eggs and vanilla. Beat well with a wooden spoon until combined. Sift in flour, baking powder, baking soda and cocoa. Mix to combine. Pour the mixture into cake tin. Bake at 180°C/Gas 4 for 45 minutes, or until cake springs back when lightly touched. Leave in tin for 10 minutes before turning onto a cooling rack. Serve with Fresh Blueberry Sauce and cream (optional).

Serves 10

important ingredients for joints and mobility

all vegetables	cherry juice	honey
watercress	lemons	fresh ginger
spinach	nuts	turmeric
beetroot	beans	rosemary
egg whites	lentils	soya beans
tuna	wholegrain bread	soya milk
salmon	wholegrain cereals	tofu
sardines	oats	tempeh
anchovies	sesame seeds	miso
shellfish	sunflower seeds	brown rice
avocado	pumpkin seeds	white rice
bananas	cider vinegar	wild rice
sour cherries	flaxseed oil	

keep 'em moving

There is an image in my head that would provide a new business opportunity for an ageing entrepreneur; it is that rest homes have been replaced by rest resorts – places to go to rest from busy, active lives. So I am starting a movement here to arm people with the knowledge they need to eat their way to joint-health so that they experience a minimum of aches and pains and can be active as they age.

Do not tell me this is unrealistic – you are talking to someone who was told in her youth that she would be in a wheelchair by the age of 25. I am already a couple of decades past that and do a 6km walk three times a week, yoga, regular Pilates classes and I love aqua aerobics. Is there anything else to say?

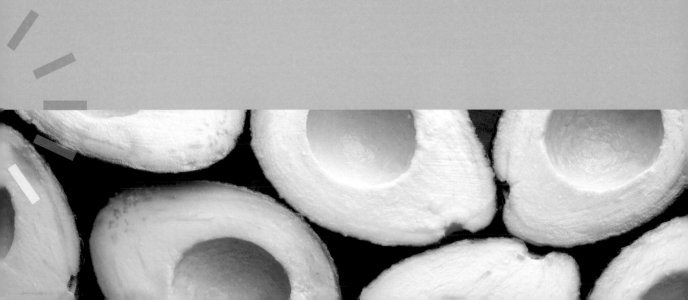

Almond and Oatmeal Hotcakes with Honeyed Bananas

For a change, try serving these delicious hotcakes with other seasonal fruit such as strawberries, blueberries and fresh crisp apples.

60g plain flour
155g oatmeal
2 teaspoons baking powder
30g ground almonds
1 egg
250ml low-fat soya milk
oil
4 small bananas
90g runny honey
natural low-fat yoghurt

Mix flour, oatmeal, baking powder and almonds together in a bowl. Lightly beat egg and soya milk together. Pour into dry ingredients and mix to combine. Cook 125ml portions of mixture in a hot, oiled pan. When golden and bubbles appear on top surface, turn and cook second side. Keep warm. Peel bananas and heat in an oiled pan or place in a dish in the microwave on High power for one minute. Serve hotcakes with banana, runny honey and yoghurt.

Serves 4

The protein, calcium and phosphorus in oats all help build strong bones and connective tissue.

The healing properties of honey help speed up recovery from joint damage and arthritis.

Don't peel your apples. Apple skins contain important flavonoids that fight inflammation.

Blueberries contain potent anti-inflammatory chemicals that help relieve arthritic pain.

Strawberries help soothe arthritic pain caused by inflammation.

Anecdotal reports tell of people suffering from arthritis-related pain gaining major relief from eating sour cherries or drinking sour cherry juice. Researchers are looking at the anti-inflammatory effect of anthocyanin pigments in cherries to see if they block the action of the enzymes that cause arthritic pain.

Bananas are one of the best sources of potassium, which helps slow the loss of calcium from the bones.

Tarzan's Joint Juice

This is a great way to start the day and, yes, it will help you swing from the trees! Make your own combination of juice in the blender or a juicer, choosing from any of these fresh fruits: cherries, banana, orange, papaya, pineapple, kiwifruit and guava. Carrot can be used, too, but is best done in a juicer. Add fresh ginger if you want an even better brew.

250ml cranberry juice
1 kiwifruit
1 large wedge papaya
1 banana

Place cranberry juice in a blender. Peel kiwifruit, papaya and banana. Chop roughly and add to blender. Blend until smooth, adding ice cubes for a well-chilled drink. Serve immediately.

Serves 1

Asian Seafood and Rice Noodle Soup

1 onion
2 cloves garlic
1 tablespoon avocado oil
1 tablespoon grated fresh ginger
1 tablespoon Thai green curry paste
1.5 litres fish stock
2 kaffir lime leaves
2 skinned and boned fish fillets
2 heads spinach
175g shelled prawns
2 tablespoons chopped fresh coriander
125g rice stick noodles
mangetout sprouts

Peel onion, halve and cut into thin slices. Crush, peel and chop garlic. Heat oil in a saucepan or clay pot. Sauté onion, garlic and ginger for 5 minutes or until soft. Add curry paste and cook for about one minute until fragrant. Add stock and bring to the boil. Cut central rib from lime leaves and slice leaves finely. Add to stock. Cut fish into chunks. Wash spinach and chop roughly. Add fish, spinach, prawns and coriander to stock and simmer for 2-3 minutes or until fish is just cooked. Cook noodles according to packet instructions. Drain and divide among four bowls. Pour fish mixture over noodles. Garnish with mangetout sprouts. Add a whole, cooked, shell-on prawn if wished.

Serves 4

Fish oils help reduce joint swelling, reducing pain for sufferers of rheumatoid arthritis.

Fresh tuna is a good food to eat to prevent and alleviate rheumatoid arthritis. It contains beneficial omega-3 fatty acids, biotin and niacin, which have an anti-inflammatory effect in the body.

Ginger has a strong anti-inflammatory effect, helping relieve arthritic pain.

Cabbage is rich in minerals, including calcium for strong bones and function of the nervous system and muscles, and magnesium, which also promotes healthy muscles.

Spinach contains calcium, magnesium and manganese – elements that help people with osteoarthritis.

Foods rich in potassium and magnesium contribute to greater bone density. Potassium is found in bananas, oranges, broccoli and papaya. Magnesium is found in dark breads, orange juice, fish, spinach, chicken and nuts.

Green Goddess and Garlic Soup

1 bunch watercress or 1 large bunch
  spinach
1 leek
4 cabbage leaves
½ iceberg lettuce
6 cloves garlic
1.5 litres chicken stock
6 sprigs parsley
1 bay leaf
1 sprig thyme
100g brown rice
wholegrain bread

Wash watercress or spinach and trim stalks if necessary. Trim leek and cut into wide slices. Cut thick core from cabbage and discard. Roughly chop cabbage and lettuce. Crush and peel garlic. Bring chicken stock to the boil in a large saucepan. Add vegetables, garlic, parsley, bay leaf, thyme and brown rice. Cover and cook for 20 minutes, or until rice is cooked. Blend or process. Serve with croûtons of toasted wholegrain bread.

Serves 4

Delicious Look-defying Lentil Salad

Now don't turn the page and say lentils aren't for you. This salad is absolutely delicious even if brown lentils don't make the top ten most appetising-looking foods. If you have a couple of sweet potatoes on hand try adding them, cooked and cubed, to this salad.

200g brown lentils
180g whole wheat
3 spring onions
1 clove garlic
1 tablespoon grated fresh ginger
1 tablespoon curry powder
2 tablespoons chopped fresh mint
4 tablespoons chopped parsley
60ml cider vinegar
⅛ cabbage
½ teaspoon salt

Wash lentils and place in a saucepan with cold water to cover. Bring to the boil and cook for 35-40 minutes or until tender. Drain and place in a bowl. Cook the precooked wheat according to packet instructions. Drain and add to lentils. Trim spring onions and cut into 1cm slices. Crush, peel and chop garlic finely. Mix spring onions, garlic, ginger, curry powder, mint, parsley and vinegar into lentil mixture. Toss to coat. Wash cabbage and shred finely. Toss through salad with salt just before serving.

Serves 6

Curcumin, the pigment that makes the turmeric used in curry powder yellow, is both a strong antioxidant and anti-inflammatory. It blocks the release of inflammatory enzymes in the cells – an action that some well-known arthritis drugs try to mimic.

The protein, calcium, magnesium, potassium and phosphorus in sweet potatoes help maintain healthy bones, muscles and nerves.

Mixing parsley, ginger, cayenne or fennel with dishes made from dried beans and lentils may help alleviate flatulence, which some people suffer as a side effect from eating these foods.

The best sources of essential fatty acids and omega-3 fatty acids are wheatgerm oil, canola oil, evening primrose oil, cod liver oil, flaxseed oil and other fish oils.

Fat is essential in the diet as it carries the fat-soluble vitamins A, D, E and K.

Salmon Puffs with Chopped Egg and Avocado

Serve these as finger food or change the bread to wholegrain toast and serve as a light meal for lunch or tea.

> 2 slices dark rye bread
> 200g can salmon
> 1 egg white
> 1 avocado
> 1 hard-boiled egg
> 2 tablespoons chopped parsley

Toast one side of rye bread. Drain salmon and remove bones. Beat egg white until stiff. Fold salmon into egg white and pile on top of untoasted side of rye bread. Grill until puffed and browned. Peel and de-stone avocado. Slice flesh into thin strips. Shell boiled egg and chop finely. Arrange avocado slices and chopped egg on bread slices. Garnish with chopped parsley.

Makes 2

Fresh Pineapple Salsa for Chicken or Fish

1 avocado
½ fresh pineapple
¼ papaya
1 tablespoon grated fresh ginger
1 tablespoon chopped fresh coriander
1 tablespoon chopped fresh mint
¼ teaspoon prepared finely chopped chilli

Peel and de-stone avocado. Chop flesh into cubes. Peel and core pineapple. Cut flesh into small cubes. Peel and de-seed papaya. Cut flesh into small cubes. Mix avocado, pineapple, papaya, ginger, coriander, mint and chilli together. Serve with grilled or steamed chicken or fish.

Makes approximately 400g

Chillies contain a chemical called capsaicin, which has a pain-relieving effect. It is helpful for general aches and pains.

Avocados contain glutathione, which helps prevent rheumatoid arthritis.

If you suffer from gout, avoid all animal foods, mushrooms, asparagus, spinach, artichokes, beans and peas. Alcohol is also off limits.

If you are overweight you increase your risk of developing osteoarthritis, particularly in weight-bearing joints. Maintaining a healthy weight will improve mobility as you age.

Banana and Cracked Wheat Muffins

45g cracked wheat
250ml boiling water
125g wholemeal flour
60g plain flour
4 teaspoons baking powder
2 teaspoons ground ginger
2 ripe bananas
85g honey
1 tablespoon avocado oil
300ml skim milk or 250ml low-fat
  soya milk and 50ml water

Place cracked wheat in a bowl. Pour over boiling water and set aside for 5 minutes. Drain. Mix wholemeal flour, plain flour, baking powder and ginger together in a bowl. Mash bananas with honey and avocado oil. Add milk or soya milk and water. Mix to combine. Make a well in the centre of the dry ingredients. Add banana mixture and cracked wheat. Mix quickly to just combine. Three-quarters fill greased American-style muffin tins with mixture. Bake at 200°C/Gas 6 for 20-25 minutes or until muffins spring back when lightly touched. Remove from oven and cover with a tea towel. Stand for 5 minutes before turning on to a cooling rack.

Makes 10

Italian Honey Nut Panforte

vegetable oil and icing sugar for cake tin
340g honey
1 tablespoon grated orange rind
2 teaspoons grated lemon rind
130g toasted almonds
40g sesame seeds, toasted
200g soft wholemeal breadcrumbs
1 teaspoon fresh rosemary leaves
½ teaspoon orange flower water

Oil a 20cm round cake tin and dust with icing sugar. Heat honey and orange and lemon rinds for 5 minutes in a saucepan large enough to mix all the ingredients. Add almonds, sesame seeds, breadcrumbs, rosemary and orange flower water. Stir continuously over a medium heat for 3 minutes or until the mixture stiffens and comes away from the sides of the saucepan. Turn into cake tin. Press the top with wet hands to smooth, but take care as the mixture will be hot. Leave until cold. Turn out and cut small wedges to serve. Store in the fridge or freezer.

Nuts have anti-inflammatory properties, which help reduce the symptoms of rheumatoid arthritis.

Sesame seeds contain high levels of vitamin E, which is essential for muscle health. A lack of vitamin E leads to muscle wastage.

important ingredients to maintain good skin

citrus fruit	yams	almonds
strawberries	sweet potatoes	walnuts
berries	mushrooms	oats
papaya	tuna	chickpeas
mango	salmon	wheatgerm
apples	sardines	wholemeal bread
kiwifruit	anchovies	soya beans
pears	oysters	soya milk
avocado	mussels	tofu
broccoli	seaweed products	tempeh
cabbage	olive oil	miso
watercress	sesame seeds	liver
spinach	sunflower seeds	garlic
pumpkin	pumpkin seeds	dark beer
peppers	lentils	brewer's yeast
carrots	Brazil nuts	
beetroot	hazelnuts	

mirror, mirror

The visible signs of ageing are probably the saddest evidence that there is a tick in that old clock. I have always thought that the sight loss that often comes with ageing is actually a kind way of preserving self-esteem. It was confirmed when I made the mistake of putting on my glasses in the full glare of an over-lit mirror. Woe is me! Is this what the rest of the world sees?

Maintaining fantastic skin is a challenge, especially for those of us who did the Sixties and Seventies version of a sun-dried tomato, baking in the sun with lashings of baby oil in pursuit of that film-star tan. Sure, some got it, but the rest of us just hoped for a freckle merger. Minimising the long-term effects of sunburn and eating foods that enhance skin health are important to how we all feel, especially as we approach and celebrate birthdays.

You may not be able to turn back the clock but you may be able to slow it by knowing what foods you can enjoy to defy the lines of time.

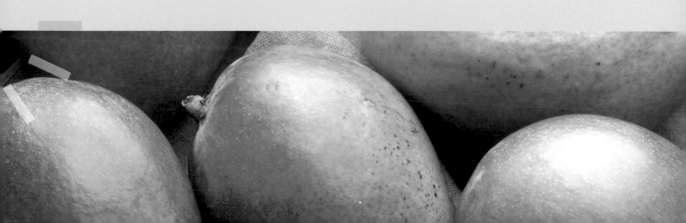

A Skinful for Breakfast

For a change, add blueberries when they are in season.

> 1 orange
> 6 strawberries
> ½ mango
> 1 slice papaya

Peel orange using a small knife, taking as much pith from the flesh as possible. Cut orange into segments between membranes. Do this over a bowl to retain juice. Hull strawberries. Cut in half if large. Add to orange slices. Peel mango and cut into slices. Peel and de-seed papaya. Cut flesh into cubes. Mix the fruit together. Place in serving bowls. Sprinkle over Oaty Topping and serve with extra juice, soya milk or yoghurt if preferred.

Oaty Topping

> 2 tablespoons Brazil nuts
> 2 tablespoons almonds
> 40g rolled oats
> 1 tablespoon wheatgerm

Finely chop Brazil nuts and almonds. Mix nuts, oats and wheatgerm together.

Serves 3

Berries contain all the essential antioxidants – vitamins A, C and E – that help prevent premature ageing. These vitamins have a cleansing function, which is great for the skin.

Blueberries are rich in anthocyanins, which give the blueberries their blue colour and oxygenate the skin to help keep it looking young and healthy.

We all know oranges are a good source of vitamin C. What is less widely known is that vitamin C is important in making collagen, which keeps the skin in good shape, defying the sagging that can come with ageing.

Soya products help build and maintain collagen and elastin in the skin, making it firm, full and youthful.

The antioxidants in spinach help reduce the risk of skin cancers.

Most nuts help maintain good skin and prevent wrinkles because they are a good source of essential fatty acids.

Roasted Mushrooms with Nutty Topping

4 large brown flat mushrooms
2 cloves garlic
1 tablespoon tahini
1 tablespoon wheatgerm
40g chopped walnuts
1 bunch spinach
2 slices wholegrain bread
120g blue cheese or feta
fresh pear slices to garnish

Wipe mushrooms and remove stalks. Trim stalks and chop finely. Crush, peel and chop garlic. Mix mushroom stalks, tahini, garlic, wheatgerm and walnuts together. Place on gill side of mushrooms. Bake, covered, at 200°C/ Gas 6 for 10 minutes. Remove cover and grill tops until golden. Wash spinach and cook in a saucepan for 3-5 minutes with just the water clinging to the leaves. Squeeze out as much water as possible. Toast bread and place one slice on each plate. Top with spinach and mushrooms. Crumble cheese over and garnish with fresh pear slices.

Serves 2

Avocado Skin-tonic Salad with Roasted Pepper Vinaigrette

2 avocados
1 roasted red pepper
1 apple
1 pear
135g roasted hazelnuts
watercress or baby spinach

Peel and de-stone avocado. Cut flesh into slices. Cut red pepper into strips. Cut apple and pear into quarters. Remove cores and slice. Mix avocado, pepper, apple, pear and hazelnuts together. Gently toss through vinaigrette. Serve on top of watercress or spinach leaves.

Roasted Pepper Vinaigrette

1 roasted red pepper
2 tablespoons lemon juice
2 tablespoons avocado oil

Place pepper, lemon juice and avocado oil in a blender or food processor and process until combined. Alternatively, sieve pepper to a purée and mix with juice and oil.

Serves 6

Avocados contain vitamin E, which strengthens collagen in the skin.

The antioxidant vitamins A, C and E and zinc are all found in peppers and there are higher levels in red peppers. Red peppers are, as a result, particularly good for the skin.

Fish oils help improve dry skin. Some claims have even been made that they reduce cellulite and help inflammatory skin conditions like dermatitis and eczema.

The essential fatty acids found in fish prevent dry skin, hair and nails. They also enhance the normal function of the reproductive system.

Salmon and Noodle Salad

125g soba noodles
200g cooked salmon fillet or smoked
   salmon
2 spring onions
½ cucumber
1 red onion
4 tablespoons fresh coriander leaves
30g fresh mint leaves
1 handful baby spinach leaves
1 handful rocket
1 handful watercress

Cook noodles according to packet instructions. Cool. Remove bones from salmon with clean tweezers and remove skin. Cut into chunks. Trim spring onions and slice finely. Cut cucumber in half lengthwise. Remove seeds and cut flesh into chunks. Peel onion and slice finely. Mix spring onions, cucumber, onion, coriander, mint, spinach, rocket and watercress together. Toss well. Arrange salad mixture on serving plates. Top with noodles and salmon. Drizzle dressing over and serve.

Dressing

½ teaspoon prepared finely chopped
   chilli
60ml avocado oil
½ teaspoon wasabi powder
1 tablespoon grated fresh ginger
125ml lime juice

Mix chilli, oil, wasabi, ginger and lime juice together until combined.

Serves 4

Steamed Mussels with Thai Spices

2 carrots
30 fresh green-lip mussels in shell
1 onion
2 cloves garlic
1 teaspoon olive oil
1-2 tablespoons Thai green curry paste
1 tablespoon Thai fish sauce
250ml orange juice
1 tablespoon shredded orange rind
2 tablespoons chopped fresh coriander

Scrub carrots, trim and cut into matchsticks. Scrub mussels, removing beards. Peel onion and chop finely. Crush, peel and chop garlic. Heat oil in a large saucepan. Sauté onion and garlic over a medium heat for 5 minutes or until soft. Add curry paste and cook for 1 minute until spices smell fragrant. Pour in fish sauce, orange juice and bring to the boil. Add carrots and cleaned mussels. Cover and cook until mussel shells open. Remove mussels as they open to prevent overcooking. Discard any mussels that do not open. Return open mussels to saucepan. Sprinkle over orange rind and coriander and serve.

Serves 2

Carrots are a valuable source of beta-carotene. This compound forms the all-important vitamin A in the body – a vitamin critical for the maintenance of the skin.

Beta-carotene, which the body converts to vitamin A, has a healing effect on the skin and improves the complexion.

Vegetables and fruit contain valuable phyto-chemicals, which play a major part in promoting health in humans. These phyto-chemicals act as powerful antioxidants and anti-inflammatories and serve as natural detoxifiers in your body.

Watercress has a reputation for being great for the skin. It helps alleviate inflammatory skin conditions such as dermatitis, eczema and psoriasis. Its antioxidant vitamins and minerals help skin health and its detoxifying power helps give skin a healthy glow.

Mushroom and Spinach Risotto

One tool I wouldn't be without is my zester. It makes it so easy to get the flavour and other advantages of citrus rind without the fuss of a grater.

If you are looking to give your skin a real boost, try serving this with a watercress salad.

1 onion
2 cloves garlic
2 tablespoons olive oil
200g arborio rice
1 litre hot vegetable stock
1 teaspoon dried thyme
1 bunch spinach
200g brown button mushrooms
1 tablespoon shredded lemon rind
1 carrot
shaved Parmesan cheese

Peel onion and chop finely. Crush, peel and finely chop garlic. Heat oil in a large frying pan. Sauté onion and garlic over a medium heat for 5 minutes or until soft. Add rice. Cook until rice looks white and opaque. Pour in hot stock, about 250ml at a time, stirring until stock evaporates before adding more. Add thyme. Wash spinach and trim stalks. Wipe mushrooms and cut in half. With last addition of stock, add spinach, mushrooms and lemon rind. Cook until stock has been absorbed and rice is cooked and creamy. Scrub carrot and grate finely. Serve on top of risotto with shavings of Parmesan cheese.

Serves 3

Indian Chicken and Mango Stir-fry

1 onion
2 cloves garlic
2 spring onions
1 carrot
¼ Chinese or savoy cabbage
1 head broccoli
410g can chickpeas
1 fresh mango
1 tablespoon sesame oil
1 tablespoon curry powder
200g chicken fillets
250ml chicken stock
1 tablespoon chopped fresh parsley or coriander
mango chutney
poppadoms

Peel onion and cut into rings. Crush, peel and chop garlic. Trim spring onions and cut into 2cm pieces on the diagonal. Scrub carrot, trim and cut into thin strips. Wash cabbage and shred finely. Wash broccoli and cut into florets. Drain chickpeas. Peel mango and cut into slices. Heat oil in a wok or frying pan. Stir-fry onion, garlic, spring onions, carrot and broccoli for 5 minutes. Add curry powder and cook for 1 minute or until spices smell fragrant. Add cabbage and chicken and stir-fry for 2 minutes or until chicken is almost cooked. Add chickpeas and chicken stock. Cook for 2 minutes or until chicken is cooked and stock hot. Serve garnished with coriander and accompanied by mango chutney and poppadoms.

Serves 4

Mangos are rich in vitamins C and E – both vitamins that are good for the skin. It also contains the carotenoid beta-cryptoxanthin, which is thought to help protect against skin damage caused by the sun. Papaya is the best source of beta-cryptoxanthin.

Mangos and papayas are like internal vacuum cleaners, detoxifying the body, resulting in improved skin texture. As well as beta-carotene they contain vitamins C and E, which are also great for maintaining good skin.

Onions, garlic and aubergine contain polyphenols, which help protect the skin.

One mango contains about 30 per-cent of our recommended daily allowance of vitamin A, 139 per-cent of vitamin C and 15 per-cent of vitamin E – all essential vitamins for skin health.

Favourite Fish with Lime, Mint and Mango Salsa

Choose your favourite fish for this dish, remembering that oily fish are better for your skin. You can use papaya if mango is not available.

300g fillet of your favourite fish
2 fresh limes
1 clove garlic
1 tablespoon Thai fish sauce
¼ cup chopped fresh mint
½ teaspoon prepared finely chopped chilli
1 kaffir lime leaf
1 mango
2 tablespoons chopped fresh coriander
tagliatelle cooked to packet instructions

Prepare fish as necessary, removing skin and bones. Cut into portion-sized pieces. Squeeze juice from limes and place in a bowl. Crush, peel and finely chop garlic. Add to juice with fish sauce, mint and chilli. Remove central vein from lime leaf and chop leaf finely. Add to bowl. Peel mango and cut into small chunks. Add to bowl with coriander and mix to combine. Grill fish for 2 minutes or until just cooked, depending on thickness of fish. Serve fish on cooked tagliatelle, topped with mango salsa.

Serves 2

Almond Apple Cake with Apple Sauce

2 eggs
150g sugar
140g plain flour
1½ teaspoons baking powder
60ml orange juice
30g slivered almonds
350g apple sauce
2 tablespoons orange marmalade

Line the base of a 20cm round cake tin with parchment paper. Beat eggs and sugar together until light and thick. Sift flour and baking powder together. Fold into egg mixture, alternately with orange juice. Spoon half the cake mixture into tin. Spoon over filling, spreading to cover cake mixture. Spread remaining cake mixture over filling. Sprinkle with slivered almonds. Bake at 180°C/Gas 4 for 45 minutes or until an inserted skewer comes out clean. Mix apple sauce and orange marmalade together. Serve cake warm or cold with apple sauce.

Filling

1 apple
130g blanched almonds, roasted and chopped
4 tablespoons orange marmalade
1 egg white

Grate unpeeled apple. Mix apple, almonds and marmalade together. Lightly beat egg white and mix into apple mixture.

Apples are rich in quercetin, which is thought to help strengthen collagen essential for youthful-looking skin.

Tea and apples contain polyphenols, which help protect the skin.

important ingredients
for a healthy heart

almonds	watercress	soya beans
pumpkin seeds	sweet potatoes	soya milk
sunflower seeds	yams	tofu
sesame seeds	garlic	tempeh
green tea	tuna	miso
celery	salmon	bananas
broccoli	sardines	apples
carrots	anchovies	pears
peppers	seaweed products	oranges
spinach	olive oil	
tomatoes	wine	

boom
ditty boom

My family has a genetic predisposition to heart disease, and having seen the demise of my dear dad to this disease, I have been determined to defy any negative heart genes I may have inherited. Genetics only has a twenty-five per-cent impact on your prognosis for life and it is twenty-five per-cent you can make sure you try to control.

Knowledge and choice make having a healthy heart a real option for those who want to get the most from life. Eating foods that will help, maintaining a healthy weight and exercising regularly are all simple and enjoyable choices to make sure you give the most important organ of your body the treatment it deserves.

Awareness of the foods that promote heart-health is the first step to making choices that will keep your ticker going 'boom ditty boom'. Incorporating these into your meal choices is easy and, believe me, it is never too late to make changes that will have a positive impact on your heart-health.

The secret is choosing foods that count – foods that taste fantastic and have a health benefit, while you enjoy a delicious eating experience.

Toasted Breakfast Muffins with Fresh Fruit

   1 apple
   1 pear
   1 orange
   1 kiwifruit
   2 passionfruit or 40ml unsweetened passionfruit pulp
   2 cinnamon-flavoured English muffins
   low-fat yoghurt or soya yoghurt
   2 tablespoons chopped hazelnuts

Wash fruit. Cut apple and pear into quarters. Remove cores and cut into thin slices. Place in a bowl. Peel orange using a small knife, taking as much pith from the flesh as possible. Cut orange into segments between membranes. Do this over the bowl the apple and pear are in to catch the juice. Peel kiwifruit and cut into chunks. Mix passionfruit pulp into fruit mixture. Slit muffins and toast. Place a muffin half on a serving plate. Top with fruit mixture. Serve with low-fat yoghurt. Sprinkle with hazelnuts.

Serves 4

Bananas and oranges are potassium-rich foods which help regulate blood pressure.

Soya products help lower high blood-pressure and cholesterol levels.

Mangos and cantaloupe melon contain the heart-helping vitamin C and folic acid, as well as potassium.

Red pigments in cranberries are thought to reduce the risk of heart-attack-inducing blood clots.

Green tea has much less caffeine than regular tea and also contains vitamins, minerals and some powerful antioxidants known as polyphenols. These antioxidants scoop up disease-causing free radicals and can help reduce blood pressure.

Eat your almonds with the skins on as the polyphenols in almond skins help prevent atherosclerosis.

Winter Fruit Salad

Use this for breakfast or dessert. It is delicious anytime. Choose dried fruits that are free of preservatives.

> 175g dried dates
> 175g dried figs
> 170g stoned prunes
> 150g sticky raisins
> 130g dried apricots
> skin of 1 orange
> 750ml hot green tea
> slivered almonds

Cut dates and figs in half if large. Place in a non-metallic bowl with prunes, raisins and apricots. Using a zester, remove thin strips of rind from the orange. (Alternatively, thinly pare the rind from the orange, avoiding the pith, and cut the rind into thin strips.) Add to fruit. Pour green tea over. Leave to soak. Cover and refrigerate until ready to serve. Serve sprinkled with slivered almonds.

Serves 8

Sweet Potato and Watercress Vichyssoise

Use spinach if watercress is unavailable.

> 1 onion
> 2 cloves garlic
> 1 tablespoon avocado or olive oil
> 2 celery sticks
> 500ml chicken stock
> 500ml miso
> 2 sweet potatoes
> 1 bunch watercress

Peel onion and chop roughly. Crush, peel and chop garlic. Heat oil in a large saucepan and sauté onion and garlic for 5 minutes or until soft. Trim celery and chop. Add to pan and sauté for 2 minutes. Add stock and miso and bring to the boil. Peel sweet potatoes and cut into pieces. Add to stock mixture. Cover and cook for 10 minutes. Wash watercress. Pureé soup in a blender or food processor with watercress. Reheat if necessary before serving.

Serves 4

Garlic improves heart-health. It can help lower cholesterol levels and high blood-pressure, and reduce clotting. It also cleanses and tones the liver.

Sweet potatoes are not just the carbohydrate fix we thought. The darker their orange colour, the more antioxidants they contain. The antioxidants they contain are vitamins A and C, and zinc. Antioxidants trap free radicals before they damage our cells.

The selenium and essential fatty acids in oily fish help protect against heart disease.

Spinach is a rich source of folic acid, which helps prevent heart disease by disposing of the amino acid homocysteine. Homocysteine is ranked by some scientists as being as significant as cholesterol and smoking in its contribution to heart disease.

Sardine Lunch Toasties

3 slices wholegrain bread
106g can sardines in tomato sauce
1 egg white
1 carrot
1 large handful baby spinach leaves
1 tablespoon lemon juice
freshly ground black pepper

Toast wholegrain bread on one side. Mash sardines. Beat egg white until soft peaks form. Fold sardine mixture into egg white. Divide mixture among bread slices, spreading on untoasted side of wholegrain bread. Grill until puffed and lightly golden. Scrub carrot and grate. Remove toast from oven. Place each slice on a serving plate. Top with baby spinach then grated carrot. Drizzle lemon juice over and grind black pepper over. Serve immediately.

Makes 3

Curried Sweet Potatoes, Banana and Broccoli Salad

3 medium sweet potatoes
1 head broccoli
4 spring onions
2 bananas
125ml lemon juice
1 tablespoon tahini
2 teaspoons curry powder
125ml avocado or olive oil
2 tablespoons chopped chives

Peel sweet potatoes and cut into pieces. Boil or steam for 15-20 minutes or until tender. Drain and cool. Cut into cubes. Place in a large bowl. Wash broccoli and cut into florets. Blanch in boiling water for 3 minutes. Drain and refresh under cold water and drain again. Add to bowl. Cut spring onions into diagonal slices. Peel bananas and cut into diagonal slices. Toss in lemon juice. Add spring onions and bananas to bowl. Mix tahini, curry powder and avocado or olive oil together. Gently mix through vegetable and banana mixture. Scatter chives over.

Serves 4

The lutein in broccoli helps protect against atherosclerosis.

The organosulphur compounds in onions and garlic are thought to be more potent than aspirin in thinning the blood, thereby helping prevent blood clots. These compounds are most potent in raw onions.

The potassium in bananas is thought to help reduce plaque formation in arteries.

Asparagus contains a flavonoid called rutin. This works with vitamin C to strengthen capillary walls.

Mushrooms, particularly strong-tasting varieties such as shitake, help reduce blood pressure and LDL-cholesterol levels. Cooking them does not reduce any of their health benefits.

Mediterranean Tart

Use this concept for other seasonal vegetables such as asparagus and mushrooms.

3 red peppers
3 yellow peppers
12 slices wholegrain bread
avocado or olive oil spray
4 tablespoons sun-dried tomato pesto
2 egg whites
½ teaspoon prepared finely chopped
   chilli
Parmesan cheese shavings
fresh basil leaves

Cut peppers in half and remove seeds. Place on an oven tray and grill until skins are blistered and black. Remove from oven. When cool enough to handle, peel off skins and cut into thirds. Remove crusts from bread. (Discard or make into soft breadcrumbs for later.) Spray slices with oil spray. With oil side out, line the base and sides of a 20cm round springform tin, overlapping the bread slices as necessary. Bake at 160°C/Gas 3 for 45 minutes or until bread is crisp. Spread base of bread case with tomato pesto. Arrange the pepper slices over the pesto. Lightly beat egg whites and chilli together to break up the egg white. Pour over peppers. Bake at 180°C/Gas 4 for 45 minutes or until egg is set. Scatter Parmesan cheese shavings over and garnish with basil leaves.

Serves 6

Mexican Beef Tortillas with Avocado Salsa

Just because you are looking after your heart doesn't mean red meat must be banished. It is still the best source of readily absorbed iron and zinc.

1 red onion
2 cloves garlic
100g piece rump steak
1 carrot
420g can mixed beans in spicy pepper sauce
140g tomato purée
125ml red wine
10 corn tortillas

Peel onion and chop finely. Crush, peel and chop garlic. Trim any fat from steak. Slice meat thinly. Scrub carrot and grate. Heat a non-stick frying pan over a medium heat and dry-fry the onion and garlic for 3-4 minutes. Add steak slices and quickly stir fry. Remove meat from pan and add beans, tomato paste and red wine. Bring to the boil, then mix in meat. Place some mixture down the centre of each tortilla. Top with grated carrot. Fold tortilla over to cover filling. Place seam-side down on an oven tray. Bake at 200°C/Gas 6 for 10 minutes or until lightly golden. Serve cut in half with Avocado Salsa.

Avocado Salsa

1 medium tomato
½ ripe avocado
1 celery stick
2 tablespoons lemon juice
freshly ground black pepper

Cut tomato into 1cm cubes, removing core. Peel and de-stone avocado. Chop flesh into cubes. Trim celery and chop finely. Mix tomato, avocado, celery and lemon juice together. Grind black pepper over.

Serves 4

The lycopene in tomatoes protects hearts and lungs from the damage caused by free radicals.

Corn offers us plenty of the B-vitamin niacin, which helps regulate cholesterol in the blood.

- Fish that have medium levels of oil include bluenose tuna, brill, blue cod, John dory, hapuka, hake, ling, monkfish, deep-sea cod, and school shark.

- Snapper has medium-to-low levels of fish oil.

- Fish with low oil content include red cod, plaice, gurnard, sole and whitebait.

- Fish oils help lower cholesterol levels and high blood-pressure, protecting the heart against disease and generally strengthening the cardiovascular system.

Steamed Fish Rolls with Sweet Chilli Sauce

250g skinned salmon, cod, tuna,
    marlin or other medium-to-
    high oil-content fish fillets
2 spring onions
2 tablespoons low-salt soy sauce
2 tablespoons lime juice
½ teaspoon prepared finely chopped
    chilli
1 tablespoon chopped fresh coriander
4 x 21cm round rice paper sheets
chives

Wash and dry fish. Cut into 2cm cubes. Trim spring onions and slice thinly. Place fish and spring onions in a bowl with soy sauce, lime juice, chilli and coriander. Mix to combine. Soak rice papers in hot water for 1 minute or until just softened. Place on a board in a single layer. Divide fish mixture evenly among sheets, placing down the centre of the sheet. Fold and roll sheets to enclose mixture. Tie with a chive. Place in a lightly oiled steamer and steam, covered, over boiling water for 4 minutes. Serve with steamed bok choy or spinach and sweet chilli sauce.

Serves 2

Orange-glazed Yams or Sweet Potatoes

For a new angle on this recipe try glazing fresh beetroot and garnish with walnuts.

    300g yams or sweet potatoes
    40ml freshly squeezed orange juice
    ½ teaspoon grated orange rind
    1 tablespoon orange marmalade
    1 tablespoon slivered almonds
    1 tablespoon shelled chopped pistachio nuts

Wash and trim yams or sweet potatoes. Boil or steam for 10 minutes or until tender. Drain. Add orange juice, rind and marmalade to yams or sweet potatoes. Heat for 2 minutes. Place in a serving bowl and sprinkle with almonds and pistachio nuts.

Serves 2

Beetroot contains a phyto-chemical called betaine, which plays a role in detoxifying homocysteine. This is particularly important when there is not enough vitamin B12 and folic acid in the diet. Sources of vitamin B12 are foods of animal origin. Sources of folic acid are lentils, asparagus, broccoli and spinach.

Oranges contain potassium, which helps lower blood pressure.

Oranges contain folic acid, which helps rid the body of homocysteine, an amino acid that has been linked to heart disease.

The linoleic acid found in walnuts helps lower cholesterol levels and blood pressure and prevent clotting.

Date, Prune and Rhubarb Loaf

250ml orange juice
4 stalks rhubarb
175g chopped dates
170g chopped stoned prunes
1 teaspoon bicarbonate of soda
60g chopped walnuts
250g wholemeal flour
1½ teaspoons baking powder

Line the base of a 23cm loaf tin with parchment paper. Pour orange juice into a saucepan large enough to mix all the ingredients. Bring to the boil. Trim rhubarb and cut into 2cm pieces. Add to orange juice. Cover and cook for 5 minutes or until rhubarb is soft. Remove from heat and cool for 10 minutes. Add dates, prunes, bicarbonate of soda and walnuts. Mix well. Add wholemeal flour and baking powder and mix to combine. Pour mixture into loaf tin. Bake at 180°C/Gas 4 for 35-40 minutes or until loaf springs back when lightly touched. Remove from oven and cover with a tea towel for 10 minutes before turning onto a cooling rack. Serve sliced with or without a thin spread of low-fat dairy-free butter substitute.

Makes 1 loaf

important ingredients
to improve cholesterol levels

olive oil	bananas	cauliflower
sesame oil	oranges	peas
safflower oil	mandarins	Brussels sprouts
sunflower oil	grapefruit	alfalfa sprouts
walnut oil	sweet cherries	onions
tuna	cranberries	garlic
salmon	avocados	oats
sardines	raisins	oat bran
anchovies	beans	soya beans
peanuts	lentils	soya milk
peanut butter	chickpeas	tofu
cashew nuts	kidney beans	tempeh
almonds	carrots	miso
apples	celery	
pears	artichokes	

the real oil

If there is one thing to put a quiver in the liver, it is the mention of cholesterol. Over the years, fear and confusion have become synonymous with cholesterol. My need to deconfuse the issue, without having to go to med school, justifies a separate chapter for this important topic.

When you have a cholesterol test you get three results: an HDL, an LDL and an overall cholesterol reading. HDL (high-density lipoprotein) cholesterol is the good cholesterol. LDL (low-density lipoprotein) cholesterol is the bad cholesterol. I remember this by calling it the lousy cholesterol. The ratio of the HDL to the LDL cholesterol gives the overall cholesterol reading.

If your LDL level is much higher than your HDL level, you have a problem. Changes in your diet can help lower your LDL cholesterol levels, thereby looking after your heart-health. If your diet relies heavily on animal and saturated plant fats and trans-fats, your LDL level will be high. Don't forget though that good cholesterol is essential for good health and our livers make cholesterol.

Raised cholesterol is usually easily controlled by diet for most people. However, if your body is over-zealous in its production of cholesterol, medication may be your only option.

My Magnificent Quick Muesli

This muesli has no added fat or sugar and still tastes great. There's nothing to break your teeth on either. However, if your muesli is going to last a while, add the cranberries as you go otherwise they dry out and become hard.

  400g wholegrain oats
  160g rolled oats
  80g oat bran
  125g flaked almonds
  75g whole linseeds
  170g dried cranberries

Place wholegrain and rolled oats, oat bran and almonds in a roasting dish. Bake at 180°C/Gas 4 for 15 minutes, mixing as necessary to ensure even cooking. Remove from oven and cool. Crush linseeds in a food processor, blender or, if you are feeling like some upper-body exercise, use a pestle and mortar. When muesli is cold mix in linseeds and cranberries and store in an airtight container. Serve with fresh fruit such as apples and pears, bananas and oranges and soya or skim milk.

Makes about 840g

We cannot digest whole linseeds so they need to be crushed or ground to make their vital nutrients available to us. They are not easy to crush so you may prefer to use ground linseeds in a recipe. I am a little sceptical about the freshness of ground linseeds and they do tend to taste a bit like munching on a cricket bat – that's why I prefer to grind my own. A clean coffee grinder or a mini food processor work well. Clean the grinder well after use to prevent the residue going rancid.

Cranberries are being researched for their role in the prevention of heart disease. The red pigments in cranberries are antioxidants, which seem to slow the oxidation of LDL (bad) cholesterol.

Grapefruit have a high vitamin C content, as well as blood pressure-lowering potassium, homocysteine-ridding folate, and cholesterol-lowering pectin. Add to this one of the best sources of D-glucaric acid, which also lowers cholesterol, and it becomes the heart-health wonder fruit. However, if you are taking prescription drugs check to see if grapefruit consumption is compatible with your medication.

Garlic is fantastic for getting rid of LDL cholesterol from the blood vessels and inhibiting the oxidation of LDL cholesterol.

Carrots are thought to lower cholesterol partly because of their fibre content and partly by inhibiting the enzyme that stimulates cholesterol synthesis.

the real oil

Carrot and Lentil Soup

1 onion
2 cloves garlic
1 tablespoon sesame oil
1.5 litres vegetable stock
2 celery sticks
4 large carrots
200g red lentils
salt
freshly ground black pepper
2 tablespoons chopped fresh coriander
   or parsley

Peel onion and chop roughly. Crush, peel and chop garlic. Heat oil in a large saucepan and sauté onion and garlic over a medium heat for 5 minutes or until soft. Pour in stock and bring to the boil. Trim celery and cut up roughly. Scrub carrots, trim ends and cut up roughly. Wash lentils. Add carrots, celery and lentils to stock. Cover and cook for 10-15 minutes or until carrots are cooked. Purée soup in a blender or, for a more coarse soup, a food processor. Season to taste with salt and pepper. Serve hot garnished with coriander or parsley.

Serves 6

Green Salad with Miso Vinaigrette

This miso vinaigrette is also delicious served with grilled aubergine.

75g mangetout
½ cauliflower
150g fresh or frozen broad beans
2 celery sticks
1 green-skinned apple
60g walnut halves, roasted, or unsalted cashew nuts, roasted
4 tablespoons chopped parsley
4 tablespoons chopped chives
mangetout sprouts

String peas and place in a heatproof bowl. Wash cauliflower and cut into small florets. Add to mangetout with broad beans. Pour over boiling water and leave for 5 minutes. Drain and refresh under cold water. Remove shells from broad beans if you are going for looks or leave shells on for their fibre benefit. Trim celery and cut into thin sticks, about 6cm long. Cut apple into quarters, remove core and slice thinly. Add celery, apple slices, nuts, parsley and chives to cauliflower mixture. Toss through Miso Vinaigrette and serve garnished with mangetout sprouts.

Miso Vinaigrette

1 tablespoon miso paste
1 teaspoon sesame oil
60ml lime juice

Mix miso paste, sesame oil and lime juice together.

Serves 4

Aubergine contains saponins, which have antihistamine, antioxidant and anti-inflammatory properties. They can also help lower cholesterol by binding with cholesterol in the gut and removing it from the body.

Don't salt aubergine before cooking because this removes the beneficial saponins from the aubergine.

Vitamins C and E, beta-carotene and selenium are found in dried and fresh fruits and fresh vegetables. These nutrients help prevent LDL cholesterol being deposited in blood vessels.

Avocados contain a phytosterol known as beta-sitosterol. It has a similar chemical structure to cholesterol and competes successfully with it for absorption in the body. The result is a lowering of cholesterol in the blood.

Polyunsaturated fats include those found in oily fish such as salmon, sardines and tuna, and in walnuts, and safflower and sunflower oils.

Smoked Salmon, Avocado and Cucumber Salad

Do not squeeze avocados to establish ripeness. The stem end will flick out of an avocado easily when it is ripe.

    100g smoked salmon slices
    1 salmon steak
    1 tablespoon horseradish sauce
    1 tablespoon fresh dill leaves
    60ml lemon juice
    1 avocado
    ½ teaspoon salt
    1 cucumber
    1 spring onion
    baby spinach leaves
    dill

Reserve 2 slices smoked salmon for garnish. Place remaining smoked salmon in the bowl of a food processor. Remove bones from salmon steak with clean tweezers. Remove skin and chop flesh roughly. Add to processor with horseradish sauce, dill and 2 tablespoons of lemon juice. Peel and de-stone avocado. Chop flesh roughly and add to salmon with salt. Process until coarsely chopped and combined.

Using a wide-blade peeler, cut long strips down the length of the cucumber to the seeds. Discard the seeds. Trim and finely slice the spring onion. Mix cucumber, spring onion and remaining lemon juice together. To serve, place baby spinach leaves on 2 serving plates. Pile salmon mixture on top of leaves. Top with cucumber salad and reserved salmon slices. Garnish with dill.

Serves 2

Warm Winter Salad with Orange and Walnut Vinaigrette

If you don't like walnuts, change the oil and nuts. Try peanuts, almonds or cashews and olive or avocado oil.

    10 Brussels sprouts
    1 large carrot
    1 red onion
    2 celery sticks
    60g walnuts

Trim Brussels sprouts. Cut a cross in the stem. Scrub carrot, trim ends and cut into matchstick pieces. Steam Brussels sprouts over boiling water for 5 minutes. Add carrot and steam for a further 3 minutes. Remove from heat. Cut Brussels sprouts into quarters and place in a bowl with carrots. Peel onion, cut in half and slice thinly. Trim celery and cut into 1cm pieces on the diagonal. Add onion, celery and walnuts to sprouts. Pour Orange and Walnut Vinaigrette over. Toss to coat.

Orange and Walnut Vinaigrette

    60ml walnut oil
    1 tablespoon tarragon vinegar
    2 tablespoons orange juice
    ½ teaspoon grated orange rind

Mix walnut oil, tarragon vinegar, orange juice and orange rind together.

Serves 4

Safflower, sunflower and walnut oils are all polyunsaturated oils, good for keeping that ratio of HDL to LDL cholesterol in check.

Research has shown that a raw onion a day can improve the ratio of HDL cholesterol and LDL cholesterol in your body, by increasing the level of HDL.

Globe artichokes contain a compound that increases the production of bile by the liver. Bile helps the body remove cholesterol. Research has shown artichokes can lower levels of LDL cholesterol, thereby giving a better ratio of good to bad cholesterols in the blood.

Monounsaturated fats include olive oil. These fats increase the level of HDL cholesterol in the body.

Artichoke Pasta with Lemon and Capers

1 onion
2 cloves garlic
1 red pepper
1 tablespoon olive oil
1 lemon
400g can artichoke hearts
50g mangetout
2 tablespoons drained capers
300g cooked drained hot pasta
soya or Parmesan cheese

Peel onion and chop finely. Crush, peel and chop garlic. Cut pepper in half. Remove seeds and cut flesh into 1cm cubes. Heat oil in a frying pan and sauté onion, garlic and pepper over a medium heat until soft. Grate rind from lemon and squeeze juice. Drain artichokes, reserving 125ml of brine. Cut artichoke hearts into quarters. String mangetout and cut in half lengthwise. Add to pan with lemon juice, rind, capers and reserved brine. Bring to the boil. Toss mixture through hot cooked pasta. Serve garnished with grated soya or Parmesan cheese.

Serves 3

Sunday Night Pizza with not a block of cheese in sight!

2 ready-made pizza bases
410g can red kidney beans
250ml stir-in tomato and chilli sauce
2 carrots
1 avocado
125ml taco sauce
alfalfa sprouts

Place pizza bases on an oven tray or hot pizza stone. Drain beans and mash lightly. Spread over pizza bases. Pour over tomato and chilli sauce. Cook at 220°C/Gas 7 for 10 minutes or until pizza base is crisp. Scrub, trim and grate carrots. Peel and de-stone avocado and chop flesh into cubes. Pile carrot on top of pizzas, top with avocado and drizzle with taco sauce. Garnish with alfalfa sprouts.

Serves 2-3

Alfalfa sprouts are a good source of saponins, which scoop up cholesterol and dispose of it from the body.

Oh, the relief! Moderate alcohol intake, regardless of the source, produces an increase in the HDL cholesterol in our bodies. And what is the definition of moderate? Sorry girls, but it's two drinks for men and one for women per day.

Oranges are not only valuable for their vitamin C content – they also promote a healthy heart. They contain a flavonoid called hesperidin which is being studied for its ability to reduce blood pressure, increase HDL cholesterol and lower LDL cholesterol.

If your LDL cholesterol levels are high avoid egg yolks, offal (liver, kidneys, etc.), squid (calamari), octopus and prawns.

Carrot, Orange and Banana Semolina Cake

Looking after your cholesterol does not have to mean missing out on sweet treats.

2 oranges
125g plain flour
1 teaspoon baking powder
1 teaspoon bicarbonate of soda
250g caster sugar
170g semolina
125ml vegetable oil
275g carrots, grated
225g banana, mashed
3 egg whites
60g dried cranberries
icing sugar

Line the base of a 20cm round cake tin with parchment paper. Place oranges in a saucepan and cover with water. Bring to the boil and simmer for 20 minutes or until oranges are soft. Drain, cool then cut into chunks removing pips. Mash with a potato masher until very fine. Mix flour, baking powder, bicarbonate of soda, sugar and semolina together in a bowl. Mix orange, oil, carrot and banana into dry ingredients until combined. Beat egg whites until stiff. Fold into cake mixture. Pour mixture into cake tin. Sprinkle over dried cranberries. Bake at 180°C/Gas 4 for 1¼-1½ hours or until cake springs back when lightly touched. Cool in tin for 10 minutes before turning on to a cooling rack.

Pear and Apple Nut Crumble

1 lemon
2 apples
2 pears

Grate rind from lemon and squeeze juice. Mix together. Grate apples and pears coarsely leaving skin on. Mix into lemon juice and rind. Place in a 1.25-litre ovenproof dish. Sprinkle over Crumble Topping and bake at 160°C/Gas 3 for 45 minutes or until golden.

Crumble Topping

120g rolled oats
2 tablespoons honey
1 tablespoon crunchy peanut butter

Mix rolled oats, honey and peanut butter together.

Serves 6

Apples contain the soluble fibre pectin. This mops up cholesterol in the digestive tract and helps dispose of it from the body. So an apple a day really will help keep the doctor away.

The soluble fibre in oats helps lower cholesterol and high blood-pressure.

Raisins are like an antioxidant powerhouse. They also contain a substance called inulin, which ferments in our guts and produces fatty acids that help lower cholesterol. Antioxidants trap free radicals before they can damage our cells.

Free radicals are like an uncontrollable child – they have little regard for the harm they cause in the body. They are electro-chemically unbalanced molecules that are made in our bodies as a result of things like cigarettes, pollution, drugs, certain foods and stress. They wreak havoc by reacting with healthy molecules, making them unstable and creating a domino effect. The result of this chain reaction is the destruction of healthy cells, which leads to disease.

the real oil

Sweet Raisin Treats

Add your favourite spices to this for a different taste.

> 1 apple
> 250g raisins
> 140g blanched whole almonds
> 40g oatmeal
> 60g ground almonds

Core apple and cut up roughly. Place in a food processor with raisins, whole almonds and oatmeal. Process until pasty and combined. Place ground almonds on a plate. Take tablespoons of mixture, roll into balls and coat with ground almonds. Store in the refrigerator.

Makes 30

important ingredients to ease menopause

kidney beans	tempeh	flaxseed oil
haricot beans	miso	linseed oil
broad beans	yams	sesame seeds
cannellini beans	sweet potatoes	pumpkin seeds
lentils	broccoli	poppy seeds
chickpeas	peas	caraway seeds
berries	beetroot	sunflower seeds
nuts	carrots	tuna
soya beans	celery	salmon
soya milk	garlic	sardines
tofu	sage	anchovies

freedom
fighting

Menopause has to be a misnomer – there is nothing too pausing about this time in a woman's or, for that matter, a man's life. Yes, men too experience menopause, albeit not as dramatically as some women.

Whilst diet may not solve all the problems of menopause, taking control of your food choices can have a major impact on the extent of the symptoms. It means making a shift in your awareness of what you eat and a conscious effort to choose foods that will benefit you at this exciting time of life.

Soya products probably make the major contribution to controlling menopause symptoms. When I discovered I had a dairy allergy I had no choice but to move my flat white from milk to soya. It is, however, a flavour you get used to, especially when you know that it is doing a good turn for your body. Foods you might not have considered before can be easily incorporated and, if necessary, disguised for those of us who don't like eating chunks of tofu or tempeh.

However, if you are already on the menopause roller coaster do not expect a miraculous change overnight. Change happens gradually so, if possible, it is best to adjust your diet before the onset of menopause to maximise the effect of diet on your body as it fights for the freedom it so rightly deserves.

Simple Sweet Rollups

These are delicious served warm for a weekend breakfast after a bowl of porridge. I use soya milk all the time for my baking, usually substituting half milk and half water for a cow's milk measure. Try making these in the food processor. It is so easy.

125g plain flour
125g plain wholemeal flour
4 teaspoons baking powder
1 tablespoon sugar
50g butter or 60ml flaxseed oil or 60ml olive oil
180ml low-fat soya milk

Mix flours and baking powder in a bowl. Mix in sugar. Melt butter and mix into dry ingredients or mix in oil. Using a fork (or in a food processor) mix in enough soya milk to make a stiff dough. Gather into a ball and roll out on a lightly floured board to form a 27 x 17cm rectangle. Spread filling over dough to within 1cm of edges. Roll up from the long side Swiss-roll style. Cut dough into 2cm slices. Place on baking tray and bake at 200°C/Gas 6 for 8-10 minutes or until cooked and lightly golden.

Filling

140g chopped dried fruit, such as dates, prunes, apricots
35g chopped nuts, such as pecans, walnuts, almonds
1 teaspoon ground mixed spice
3 tablespoons runny honey or maple syrup

Mix dried fruit, nuts, mixed spice and honey or maple syrup together.

Makes 9

Linseed, also known as flaxseed, contains omega-3 fatty acids. It also contains lignans, which are phyto-estrogens. These lignans alter the balance of oestrogen in the body so don't overdose on the linseed. Two or three tablespoons a day is enough as the husks are toxic in high doses.

Replace tea, coffee and sweetened fizzy drinks with herbal or fruit teas, sugar-free juices, cordials and water. Fruit-based drinks make a good substitute on alcohol-free days.

Oats help stabilise oestrogen levels and reduce water retention.

There is always a concern about reduced bone density after menopause. Knowing that the calcium from animal sources is rapidly absorbed but more easily lost from the body is important. That is why vegetable sources of calcium become more important. Although they are less easily absorbed, they are retained longer.

Sage is thought to help reduce hot flushes. Try using it to make a fresh herb tea.

Sweet Potato, Pumpkin and Split Pea Soup with Sesame Sage Pesto

2 onions
4 cloves garlic
500g piece pumpkin
1 sweet potato
1 tablespoon olive oil
2 tablespoons miso paste
500ml cold water
200g yellow split peas
1 litre cold vegetable or chicken stock

Peel onions and chop finely. Crush, peel and chop garlic. Peel pumpkin and de-seed. Cut into chunks. Peel sweet potato and cut into chunks. Heat oil in a large saucepan. Sauté onion and garlic for 5 minutes or until clear. Stir miso paste into water. Add pumpkin, sweet potato, split peas, stock and miso to the saucepan. Cover and bring to the boil. Simmer for 30-40 minutes or until vegetables are soft and peas tender. Mash to break up pumpkin and sweet potato. Serve hot garnished with Sesame Sage Pesto.

Sesame Sage Pesto

60g sage leaves
60ml safflower oil
1 tablespoon sesame oil
2 teaspoons toasted sesame seeds

Place sage leaves in a food processor. Process to chop. Add oils and sesame seeds and process until combined but still coarse.

Makes about 60ml

Serves 6

Savoury Tarte Tatin

1 large sweet potato
125g plain flour
2 teaspoons baking powder
fresh sage

Peel sweet potato and cut into chunks. Cook in boiling water for 10 minutes or until soft. Reserve 125ml cooking water. Mash sweet potato in cooking water and leave to cool. Mix in flour and baking powder to form a stiff, manageable dough, adding more flour if necessary. Wrap in cling film and refrigerate while preparing the topping. Roll or press dough out to size of pan used for topping on a piece of parchment paper. Carefully lift to cover topping mixture in pan. Return to heat and cook over a medium heat for 10 minutes. Place pan under a hot grill and cook sweet-potato base until golden. Run a knife around edge of pan to loosen tatin and turn onto a serving plate. Serve garnished with fresh sage.

Topping

6 shallots
8 cloves garlic
250g tofu
2 medium-sized fresh beetroot
1 tablespoon olive oil
2 tablespoons pepper relish
1 tablespoon hot water

Peel shallots and cut into halves. Peel garlic, leaving cloves whole. Cut tofu into 1cm wide chip shapes. Trim beetroot and peel. Cut into 1cm wedges. Heat olive oil in a 24cm frying pan with an ovenproof handle. Sauté onion, garlic and beetroot over a medium heat for 5 minutes. Remove from heat. Spread evenly over base of pan and arrange tofu on top. Mix pepper relish and water together and pour over mixture in pan.

Serves 4

Beetroot is a powerful antioxidant and de-toxifier and is therefore a beneficial food to include before and during menopause to help alleviate its symptoms.

Tofu contains large quantities of calcium thanks to the calcium compounds used in its processing. Calcium is important for maintaining healthy bones, particularly after menopause.

Carrot and Poppy Seed Salad

2 carrots
1 tablespoon poppy seeds
2 tablespoons chopped parsley
1 lemon

Scrub carrots and grate. Mix carrot, poppy seeds and parsley together. Squeeze over the juice from the lemon and toss to coat.

Broccoli and carrots seem to have a major impact on the health of just about every organ in the body. They have a powerful cleansing effect on the liver, which is the major de-toxifying organ in the body. Use carrots as a snack in a pre- and during-menopause regime for a healthy liver and good sustained energy supply.

Phyto-estrogens (oestrogens from plants) improve moistening, cooling and lubricating functions in the body, helping to alleviate hot flushes and keep other important body functions fully operational.

Bananas contain vitamin B6, which may help alleviate menopause-related problems. They help to produce amino acids that control mood. Broccoli, kidney beans and bananas are also good sources of vitamin B6.

Middle Eastern Broccoli Crustless Quiche with Carrot and Poppy Seed Salad

2 onions
2 cloves garlic
1 head broccoli
4 eggs
4 tablespoons hummus
60g plain flour
250ml low-fat soya milk
125ml water
1 teaspoon prepared finely chopped chilli
½ teaspoon salt
freshly ground black pepper
2 tablespoons pine nuts or chopped walnuts

Peel onions and chop finely. Crush, peel and chop garlic. Dry fry onion and garlic in a non-stick pan for 5 minutes or until onion is clear. Wash broccoli and cut into florets. Place eggs, hummus, flour, soy milk, water, chilli, salt, pepper and broccoli florets into the bowl of a food processor and process until combined and broccoli is coarsely chopped. Mix in onion and garlic. (Alternatively, chop broccoli coarsely and beat ingredients with a whisk instead of using a food processor.) Pour mixture into a 20cm quiche dish. Sprinkle with nuts. Bake at 180°C/Gas 4 for 45 minutes or until mixture is set. Serve hot or cold with Carrot and Poppy Seed Salad.

Serves 6

Warm Soba Noodle Lamb and Steamed Vegetable Salad with Sesame Ginger Dressing

200g lean boneless lamb, such as fillets
100g mangetout
300g asparagus
2 cloves garlic
3 spring onions
4 large brown mushrooms
1 teaspoon sesame oil
125g soba noodles
mangetout sprouts

Trim any fat or sinew from lamb fillets. Trim and string mangetout. Break tough ends from asparagus and trim to neaten. Cut spears in half on the diagonal. Crush, peel and chop garlic. Trim spring onions and cut into 1cm slices on the diagonal. Wipe mushrooms and slice. Heat sesame oil in a frying pan and sauté garlic and spring onions for 2 minutes. Add mushrooms and stir-fry for 1 minute. Remove from heat. Grill lamb fillets for 1-2 minutes or until still pink in the middle. Rest for 5 minutes. Place asparagus and mangetout in a steamer and cook over boiling water for 3-5 minutes. Cook noodles in boiling water for 3 minutes or according to packet instructions. Drain well. Divide among 4 serving bowls. Cut lamb into 0.5cm thick slices. Toss lamb, vegetables, mushroom mixture and Sesame Ginger Dressing together and serve over noodles. Garnish with mangetout sprouts.

Sesame Ginger Dressing

2 tablespoons grated fresh ginger
2 tablespoons tahini
1 tablespoon flaxseed oil or olive oil
60ml white vinegar
3 tablespoons soy sauce

Place ginger, tahini, oil, vinegar and soy sauce in a screw-top jar. Shake to combine.

Serves 4

Wherever there is fat in an animal food there is oestrogen. Removing as much animal fat as possible from our diet will reduce the influence of these unwanted oestrogens.

Yams help stabilise oestrogen levels and help mood swings and other menopause-related problems.

An imbalance in hormones will accentuate menopause symptoms. Diet can play a significant part in helping balance hormone levels.

Oily fish, such as tuna and salmon, feature heavily in all aspects of anti-ageing health.

Japanese-style Fish Kebabs

400g boneless fresh tuna, salmon or
    other oily fish
3 cloves garlic
1 tablespoon finely grated fresh ginger
2 tablespoons red miso paste
¼ teaspoon smoked paprika
¼ cup mirin
2 celery sticks
120g mesclun
1 sheet toasted nori
1 teaspoon sesame oil
2 tablespoons mirin
2 tablespoons pickled ginger

Cut fish into 2cm cubes and place in a shallow dish. Crush, peel and finely chop garlic. Mix garlic, ginger, miso, paprika and first measure of mirin together. Pour over fish. Set aside for 15-20 minutes. Thread fish on to eight skewers or bamboo satay sticks. Trim celery and cut into thin sticks on the diagonal. Wash and dry mesclun. Shred nori finely. Toss celery and nori through mesclun. Cook kebabs for 2 minutes or until just cooked. Arrange mesclun on serving plates. Mix sesame oil, second measure of mirin and any residual marinade together. Place kebabs on top of mesclun, drizzle with sesame oil mixture and serve with pickled ginger.

Serves 4

Stir-fried Vietnamese Beef

Having the steak partly frozen makes it easier to slice thinly.

   1 onion
   2 cloves garlic
   300g piece topside or rump steak
   1 red pepper
   1 head broccoli
   2 celery sticks
   4cm long piece fresh ginger
   1 carrot
   1 tablespoon groundnut oil
   1 teaspoon sesame oil
   4 tablespoons black bean sauce
   60ml water
   60g fresh mint leaves
   30g fresh coriander leaves

Peel onion and cut into rings. Crush, peel and chop garlic. Thinly slice topside or rump steak. Cut pepper in half. Remove seeds and cut flesh into thin strips. Wash broccoli and cut into florets. Trim celery and cut into thin strips. Peel ginger and cut into thin strips. Scrub carrot and grate coarsely. Heat oils in a wok or large frying pan. Sauté onion and garlic for 2-3 minutes. Stir-fry meat in batches for 30 seconds-1 minute or until almost cooked. Remove each batch from wok or pan and set aside. Add broccoli to wok. Stir-fry one minute. Add pepper, celery and ginger and stir-fry for 2 minutes. Return meat to pan and mix in black bean sauce and water. Bring to the boil. Toss through carrot, mint and coriander leaves and serve with steamed rice.

Serves 4

Three servings of broccoli a week can be beneficial for people suffering depression. The folic acid in broccoli promotes the production of serotonin. This is a mood-lifting chemical that is found at only low levels in people suffering from depression. Depression and mood swings can be a side effect of menopause.

Fats in the diet are essential because they make up many necessary parts of our bodies. These include hormones and nerve coverings.

- Soya products, chickpeas, dried beans and lentils are all rich in phyto-estrogens.

- Our bodies have oestrogen receptors on to which oestrogen attaches. At menopause, when oestrogen levels change, many of these receptors can fill up with oestrogen, if there is an oversupply, or they are left unfilled, if there is an undersupply. Either way, the effect is dramatic. The best way to overcome this problem is to make changes in your diet, preferably before menopause, to include foods that contain phyto-estrogens.

- Phyto-estrogens are about 100 times weaker than other oestrogens, yet they are taken up by the oestrogen receptors helping to keep the body in oestrogen balance. A diet rich in phyto-estrogens for men and women is the best way to avoid the nasty side affects of menopause.

Delicious White Bean Mash

Use haricot beans for this if you have time to cook from scratch. Soak the beans for a couple of hours. Drain and cook with plenty of stock and the other flavourings for 40-45 minutes or until tender. If using canned beans, check the list of ingredients – you do not want beans with added sugar or salt.

  1 onion
  2 cloves garlic
  250ml vegetable stock
  1 bay leaf
  2 sprigs sage
  2 celery sticks with tops on
  410g can butter beans
  avocado oil

Peel onion and chop finely. Crush, peel and chop garlic. Place onion, garlic, stock, bay leaf, sage and celery sticks in a saucepan. Cover and bring to the boil. Reduce heat and simmer for 5 minutes. Add beans and simmer for 5 minutes. Remove bay, sage and celery and discard. Mash beans with a potato masher. Serve drizzled with a little avocado oil as a vegetable accompaniment.

Serves 2-3

New York Cheesecake

Chances are your friends are at the same stage in life as you so why not look after everyone's wellbeing when entertaining? I'm not big on eating chunks of tofu but this is an excellent way to gain the advantages of eating soya without compromising texture or taste, and it will impress at your next dinner party.

Base

14 digestive biscuits
70g blanched almonds
  or ground almonds
50g butter

Filling

500g soft curd tofu
100g caster sugar
2 tablespoons lemon juice
2 tablespoons grated lemon rind
4 eggs
1 teaspoon vanilla essence
250ml low-fat soya milk

Place biscuits and almonds in the bowl of a food processor and process until fine crumbs. Alternatively, crush biscuits and mix with ground almonds. Melt butter and mix into crumb mixture until combined. Press into the base of a 20cm springform tin. Place tofu in the bowl of a food processor and process until smooth. Add sugar, lemon juice, rind, eggs, vanilla and soy milk. Process until combined. (Alternatively, sieve tofu and beat with remaining ingredients until smooth.) Pour filling over base and bake at 160°C/Gas 3 for 1¼ hours or until set. Turn oven off but leave cheesecake in oven for a further 15 minutes. Remove from oven and allow to cool. Serve with a Raspberry Coulis and fresh berries.

Raspberry Coulis

250g fresh or frozen raspberries
2 tablespoons icing sugar

Process, blend or sieve raspberries. Sieve purée to remove seeds if using a processor or blender. Mix in icing sugar to taste.

Serves 8-10

important ingredients
for a healthy prostate

sunflower seeds	broccoli	apples
sesame seeds	bok choy	oysters
pumpkin seeds	cauliflower	mussels
Brazil nuts	watermelon	soya beans
tomatoes	pink grapefruit	soya milk
cabbage	guava	tofu
mushrooms	papaya	tempeh
onions	apricots	miso
Brussels sprouts	cranberries	

little jack horner

After what sometimes seems a life sentence being a woman, there is always a slight satisfaction when the men in our lives have to go and have their prostate checked.

There was a worldwide hurricane when all the men sighed with relief at the introduction of a blood test for checking prostate health. Sorry, boys, but it has been found to be unreliable. The digital method is still the most reliable way to check prostate function. (I think that must have been decided by a woman.) It is good to take preventative measures to ensure those tests always return a negative result.

It is so easy to incorporate foods in an everyday diet that will give a man the best shot at maintaining a healthy prostate. So, fellas, take a grip on yourselves and make sure you, or whoever makes the food choices in your household, incorporate foods for prostate protection on a regular basis. And girls, just remember we have a vested interest in this too!

Roasted Tomato, Carrot and Pepper Soup

2kg tomatoes
2 onions
4 cloves garlic
2 carrots
2 red peppers
1 teaspoon prepared finely chopped chilli
500ml vegetable stock
1 small savoy cabbage leaf
avocado oil
toasted wholegrain bread

Cut a cross in the stem end of the tomatoes. Place in an ovenproof dish. Peel onions and cut into quarters. Place in dish with tomatoes. Wash unpeeled garlic. Add to dish. Scrub carrots and cut in half lengthwise. Add to dish. Cut peppers in half. Remove seeds and place cut-side down in dish. Bake vegetables at 200°C/Gas 6 for 40 minutes. Remove from oven and peel off tomato skins. Squeeze garlic from skins. Put tomatoes, garlic, roasted vegetables and chilli in the bowl of a food processor or blender and process until smooth. Pour into a saucepan. Add a little stock to processor or blender and process to remove vegetable residue. Pour into saucepan with the rest of the stock. Bring to the boil. Roll cabbage leaf up tightly and shred very finely. Serve soup garnished with cabbage shreds and a drizzle of avocado oil and with fingers of toasted wholegrain bread.

Serves 6-8

Tomatoes contain the potent and powerful antioxidant lycopene. Lycopene tends to collect in the lungs and prostate. Where it collects it tends to decrease the development of cancer.

Other sources of lycopene are watermelon, guavas, papaya and pink grapefruit.

Broccoli, cabbage, Brussels sprouts and cauliflower have all been found to reduce the risk of prostate cancer.

Diets that are high in fat increase the amount of oestrogen and testosterone the body produces. High levels of these hormones can trigger the growth of tumours in the prostate.

Jack's Slaw

To roast sunflower seeds, place seeds in a frying pan over a low heat. Shake pan regularly until seeds start to colour.

**¼ Chinese or savoy cabbage
1 red onion
2 celery sticks
1 apple
60g dried apricots, finely sliced
4 tablespoons sunflower seeds, roasted**

Wash cabbage and shred finely. Peel onion and cut into thin slices. Trim celery and cut into 0.5cm slices on the diagonal. Cut apple into quarters, leaving skin on. Core and slice thinly. Mix cabbage, onion, celery, apple and apricots in a bowl. Pour over dressing and toss to coat. Garnish with toasted sunflower seeds.

Dressing

**1 tablespoon red miso paste
1 teaspoon prepared Dijon mustard
1 teaspoon Tabasco sauce
2 tablespoons white vinegar
2 tablespoons safflower oil
1 teaspoon sesame oil**

Place miso paste, mustard, Tabasco, vinegar, safflower and sesame oils in a screw top jar. Shake to combine.

Serves 6

Steamed Greens with Seedy Sprinkle

1 head broccoli
3 celery sticks
1 bunch spinach
8 small Brussels sprouts

Wash broccoli and cut into florets. Trim celery and cut into serving-sized pieces. Wash spinach and trim stalks. Trim Brussels sprouts. Place broccoli in a steamer and cook over boiling water for 5 minutes. Add celery and Brussels sprouts to steamer and cook for 3 minutes. Add spinach and cook for 1 minute. Remove from steamer and toss vegetables together. Sprinkle over 2 tablespoons Seedy Sprinkle and serve.

Serves 6

Seedy Sprinkle or Dukkah Dipper

4 tablespoons poppy seeds
2 tablespoons linseed
2 tablespoons sesame seeds
2 tablespoons pumpkin seeds
1 tablespoon fennel seeds
1 teaspoon ground cumin
1 teaspoon ground coriander
1 teaspoon grated lemon rind

Place all the seeds in a food processor or clean coffee grinder and process until crushed. This makes the nutrients stored in the seeds able to be used by the body. Mix in cumin, coriander and lemon rind. Store in an airtight container in the fridge.

Makes about 75g

Pumpkin seeds contain B vitamins, calcium, iron, magnesium and zinc, all of which help prostate health.

Sesame seeds contain high levels of vitamin E, folic acid, calcium, selenium, iron, magnesium and zinc.

Eating raw tomatoes is not the secret to increasing the lycopene levels in your body. Cooking tomatoes, especially with a little oil, helps release the lycopene from the fibres of the cell walls in the tomato. Lycopene is fat soluble so adding a little oil in the cooking process helps transport the lycopene, making it available to the body.

In some European countries, pumpkin seeds have been used as a remedy for benign enlargement of the prostate.

Moroccan Chicken Casserole

2 onions
4 cloves garlic
1 tablespoon avocado oil
200g red lentils
6 skinned and boned chicken thighs
140g tomato purée
400g can chopped tomatoes
½ teaspoon harissa paste or to taste
500ml chicken stock
85g pitted prunes
60g dried apricots
2 tablespoons chopped parsley
3 tablespoons chopped pumpkin seeds

Peel onions and chop finely. Crush, peel and chop garlic. Heat oil in a pan and sauté onion and garlic over medium heat for 3 minutes. Wash lentils. Place in the bottom of a 2.5-litre ovenproof casserole. Place chicken on top, making sure all fat is removed. Add tomato purée and onion to tomatoes and harissa paste. Mix to combine. Pour chicken stock into casserole, then pour over tomato mixture. Cover and cook at 180°C/Gas 4 for 1 hour. Add prunes and apricots. Cover and cook for a further 40 minutes. Mix parsley and pumpkin seeds together. Sprinkle over casserole and serve.

Serves 6

Steamed Fish Parcels with Bok Choy and Oyster Sauce

If you have individual bamboo steamer baskets, use these instead of wrapping the fish in paper.

2 fillets white-fleshed, skinned and boned fish
2 small heads bok choy
1 celery stick
2 spring onions
2 large brown mushrooms
2 tablespoons oyster sauce

Wash and dry fish and cut into 2cm-wide crosswise strips. Wash bok choy, trim and cut in half lengthwise. Place each bok choy in the centre of a piece of greaseproof paper. Divide fish pieces, placing half on top of each bok choy. Trim celery and cut into 2cm-long pieces on the diagonal. Trim spring onions, cut in half and cut into thin lengthwise strips. Trim mushrooms and slice thinly. Place half the celery, spring onions and mushrooms on top of each parcel. Spoon half the oyster sauce over each mixture. Wrap paper around fish mixture into a tight package. Place on a rack over a pan of boiling water. Cover and steam for 5 minutes or until fish is cooked. To serve, cut paper in a cross shape to reveal contents. Serve with steamed brown or white rice. If using bamboo steamers, cover with the lid and steam over boiling water in a wok or frying pan.

Serves 2

Fish is one of the better sources of selenium, which helps protect against prostate cancer. Selenium attacks free radicals and removes heavy metals like mercury from the body.

Mushrooms are a good source of selenium (among other things) and are therefore good for prostate-health.

When cooking vegetables, always put them into boiling, unsalted water or, better still, steam them to retain as many nutrients as possible. A little water and short cooking times will give you the most nutrients from your vegetables if you must boil them. Adding salt to the cooking water leaches out valuable nutrients during cooking by drawing water from the vegetables. Use salt sparingly and add after cooking if you must.

Vegetable Curry

¼ cauliflower
1 head broccoli
8 Brussels sprouts
12 asparagus spears or green beans
200g piece pumpkin
2 onions
4 cloves garlic
1 tablespoon avocado oil
1 tablespoon hot curry powder
2 x 400g cans chopped tomatoes
2 cups vegetable stock
2 tablespoons tomato purée
1 teaspoon salt
1 tablespoon chopped fresh coriander

Wash cauliflower and broccoli and cut into florets. Cut Brussels sprouts in half. Break woody ends from asparagus and cut spears in half. If using beans, top and tail, string and cut in half. Peel and de-seed pumpkin. Cut into cubes. Peel onions and cut into 0.5cm slices. Crush, peel and chop garlic. Heat avocado oil in a saucepan large enough to cook all the vegetables. Sauté onion and garlic over a medium heat for 5 minutes. Add curry powder and cook for 1 minute or until spices smell fragrant. Add tomatoes, vegetable stock, tomato purée and salt to saucepan and bring to the boil. Add pumpkin and cook for 5 minutes. Add cauliflower, broccoli, Brussels sprouts and asparagus or beans and cook for 10-15 minutes or until vegetables are tender. Serve hot, garnished with coriander.

Serves 6

Fruit Betty

Leftovers, if you are lucky enough to have any, are great for breakfast.

60g dried apricots
125ml boiling water
3 apples
410g can guavas
60g dried cranberries
2 teaspoons grated lemon rind
100g fresh wholemeal breadcrumbs
40g brown sugar
35g Brazil nuts, chopped

Put apricots in a bowl. Pour over boiling water and set aside while preparing remaining ingredients. Cut apples into quarters, remove cores and cut each quarter into five slices. Arrange in a 2-litre ovenproof dish or six 250ml ovenproof dishes. Drain guavas (use juice for something else) and cut in half if large. Arrange over apples. Place undrained apricots in dish with fruit. Sprinkle over cranberries. Mix lemon rind, breadcrumbs, sugar and Brazil nuts together. Sprinkle crumb mixture over fruit. Bake at 180°C/Gas 4 for 35 minutes or until apples are soft and crumbs are lightly golden.

Serves 6

Brazil nuts are rich in selenium. High intakes of selenium have been linked to low rates of prostate cancer.

It only takes one Brazil nut to get all the selenium you need for a day.

Spiced Nuts
To Serve with Drinks

140g Brazil nuts
115g hazelnuts
140g blanched almonds
140g cashew nuts
110g pecans
4 tablespoons Thai red curry paste
1 sheet toasted nori

Put nuts in a bowl. Add curry paste and toss nuts to coat evenly. Turn into a roasting tin and roast nuts at 180°C/Gas 4 for 15-20 minutes or until nuts are lightly golden. Cool. Roll nori tightly. Cut down the centre lengthwise. Stack nori pieces and shred finely. Mix through nuts. Store in an airtight container until ready to serve.

Makes aboufs 650g

The phyto-estrogens in soya products help protect against hormone-related cancers such as prostate cancer.

Avocado and Smoked Salmon Pâté
To Serve with Drinks

1 clove garlic
1 avocado
100g smoked salmon pieces
125g tofu
1 tablespoon tomato purée
½ teaspoon prepared finely
    chopped chilli
1 small tomato
1 tablespoon chopped parsley
wholegrain toast

Crush and peel garlic. Peel and de-stone avocado. Chop flesh roughly. Place garlic, avocado, salmon, tofu, tomato paste and chilli in a food processor or blender and process until smooth. Pile into a dish. Finely chop tomato. Mix with parsley. Place on pâté. Serve with wholegrain toast.

Makes about 350g

index